Shining Mandala

Copyright: Published in the United States by Fred Sanchez
Published December 2016
ISBN-13: 978-1541256415
ISBN-10: 1541256417

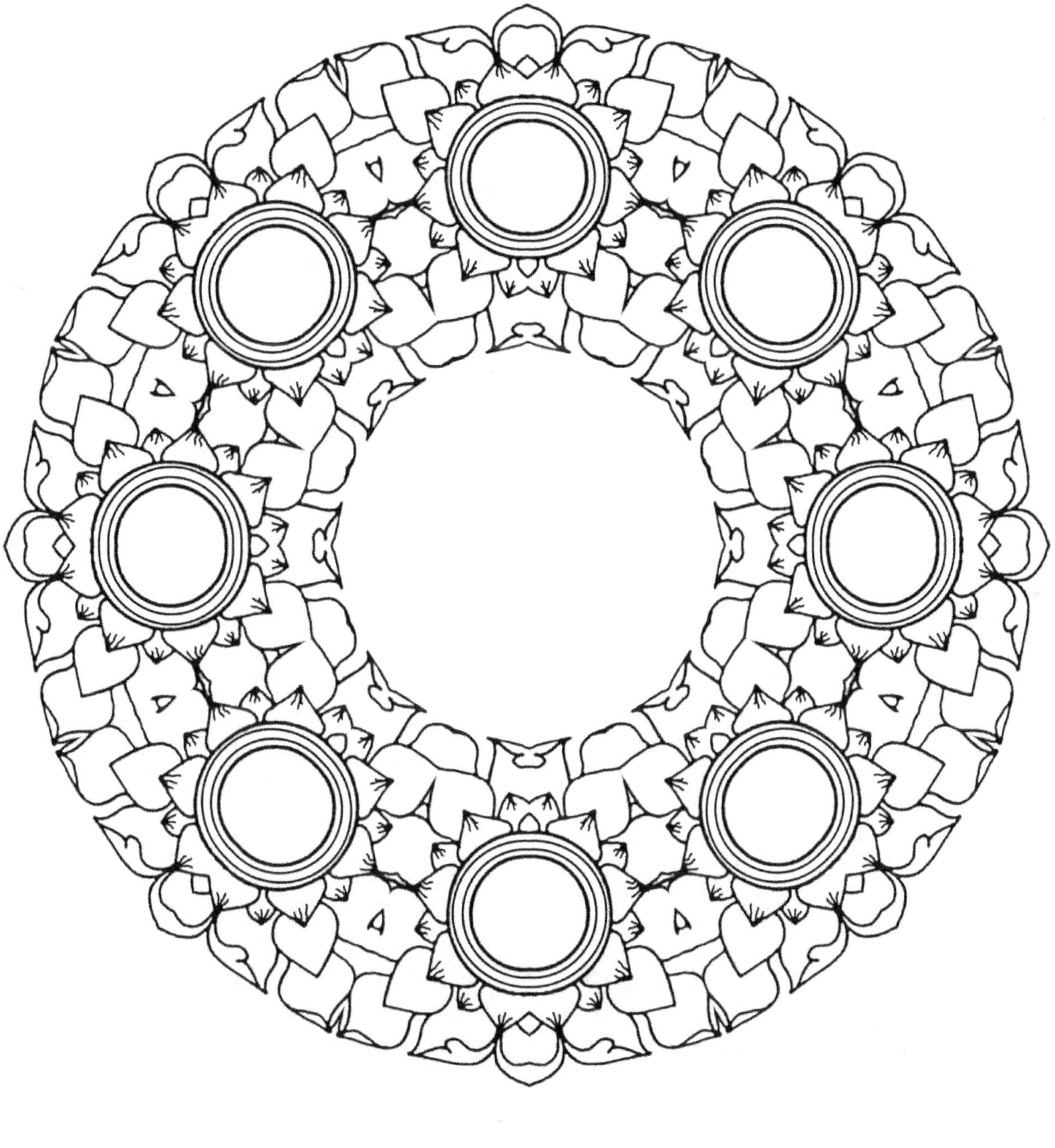

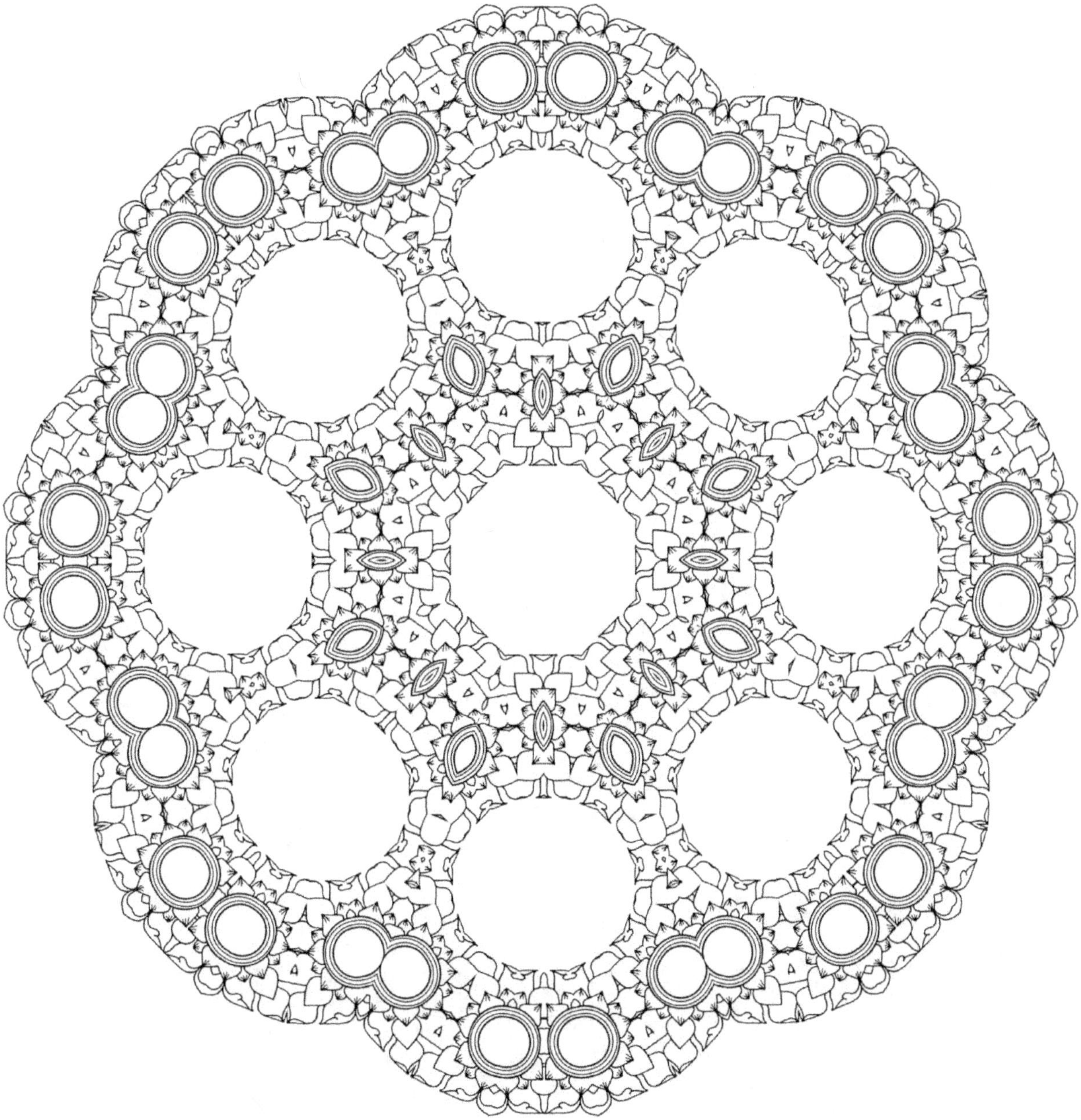

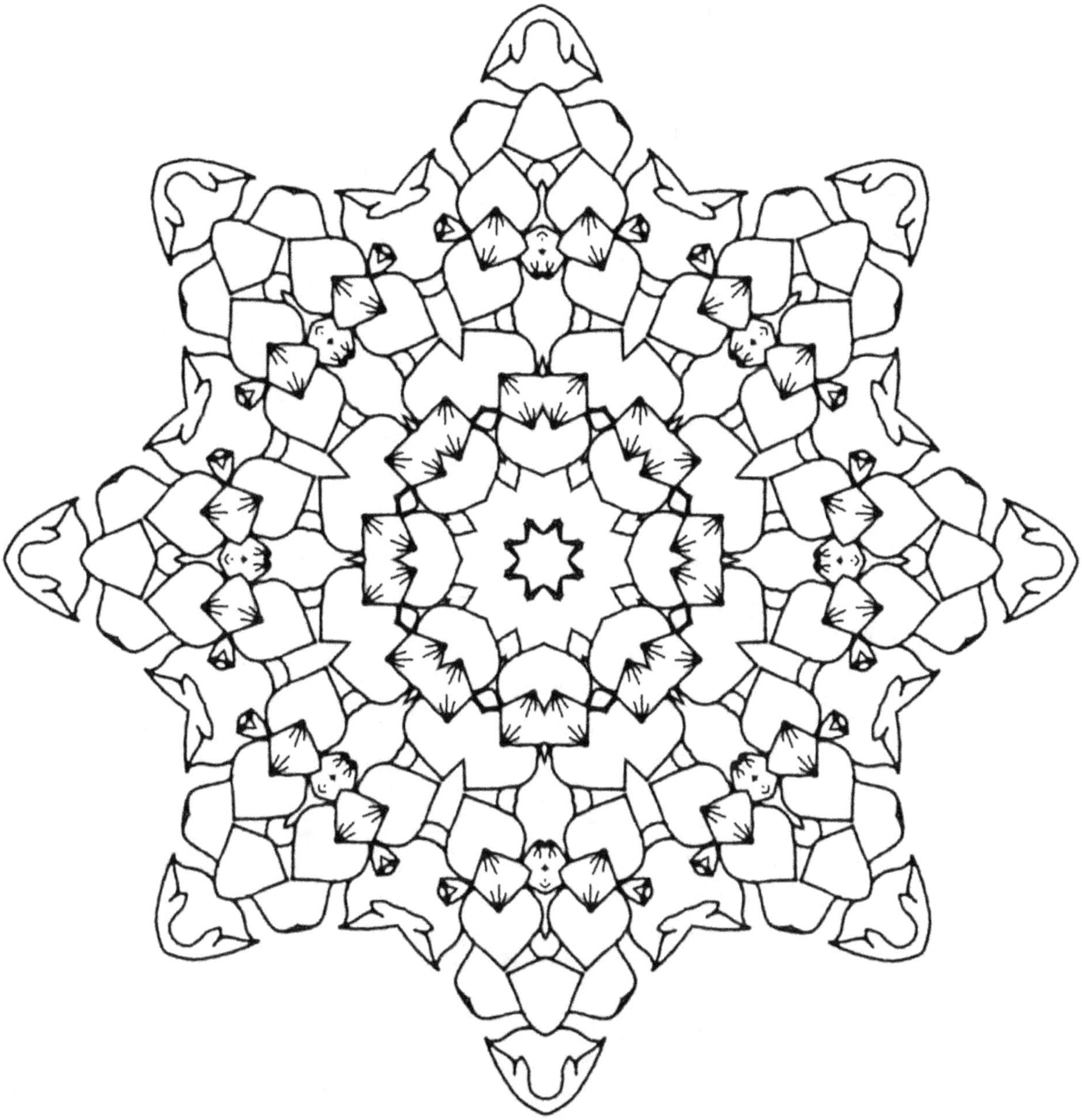

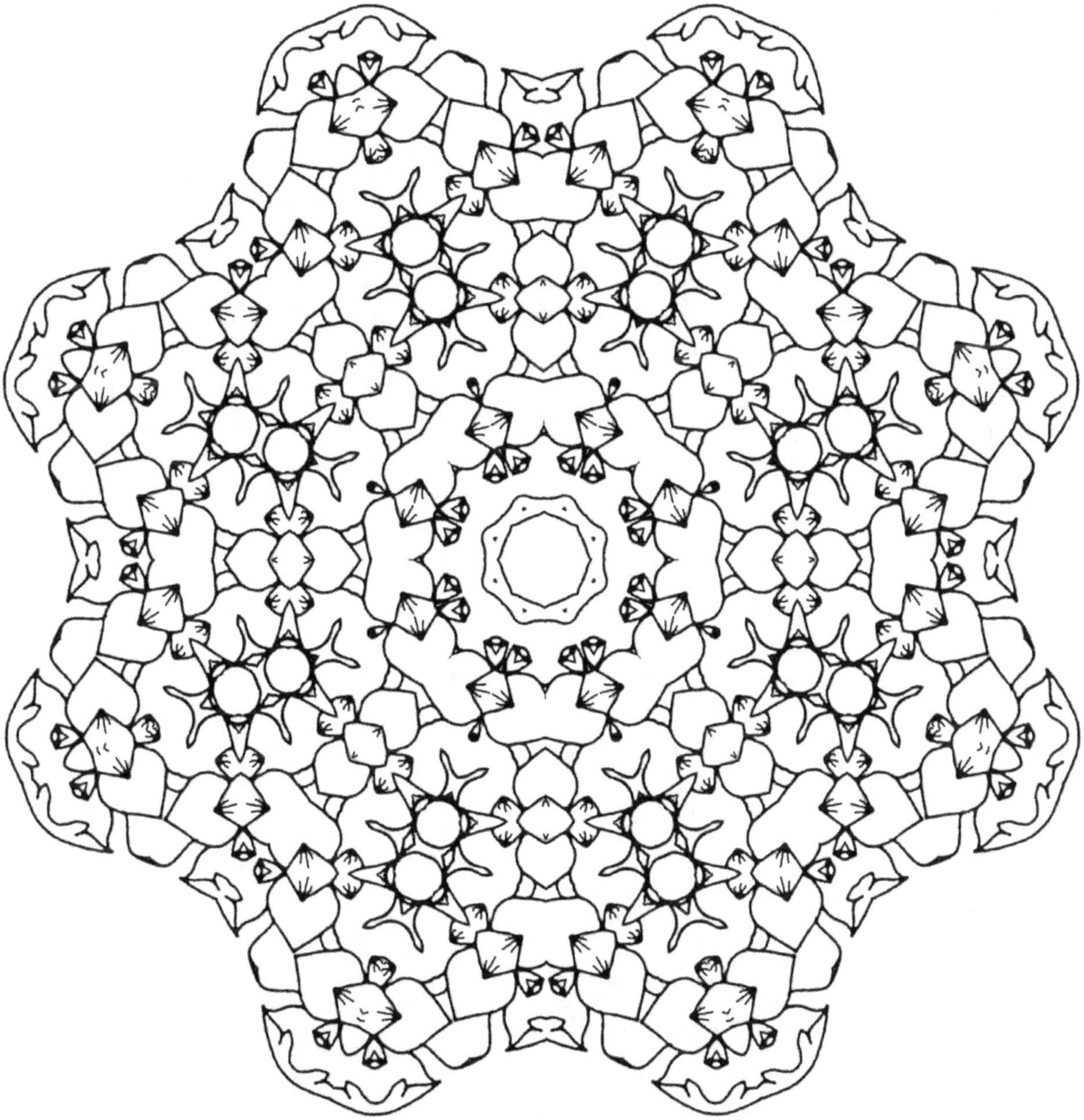

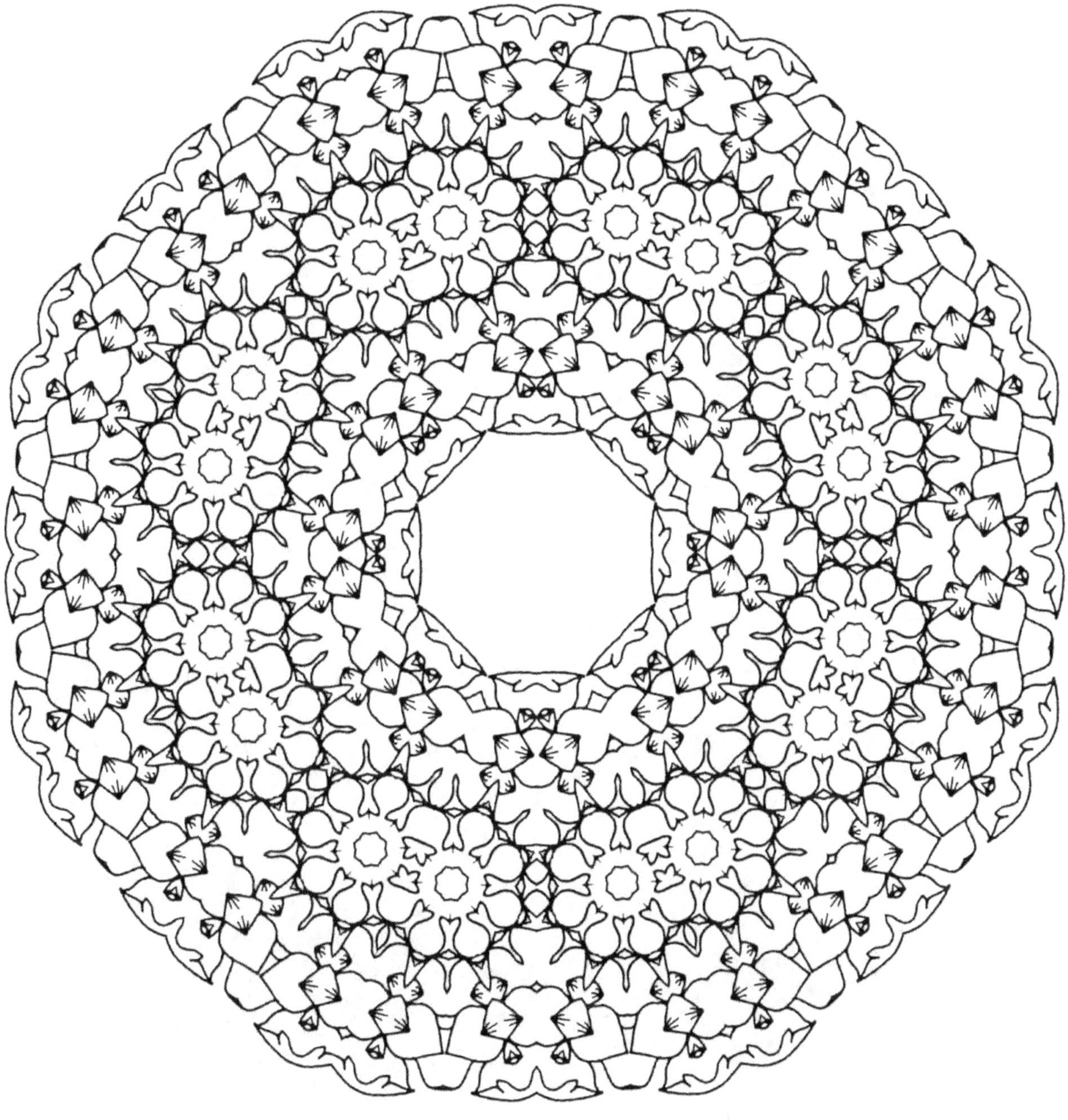

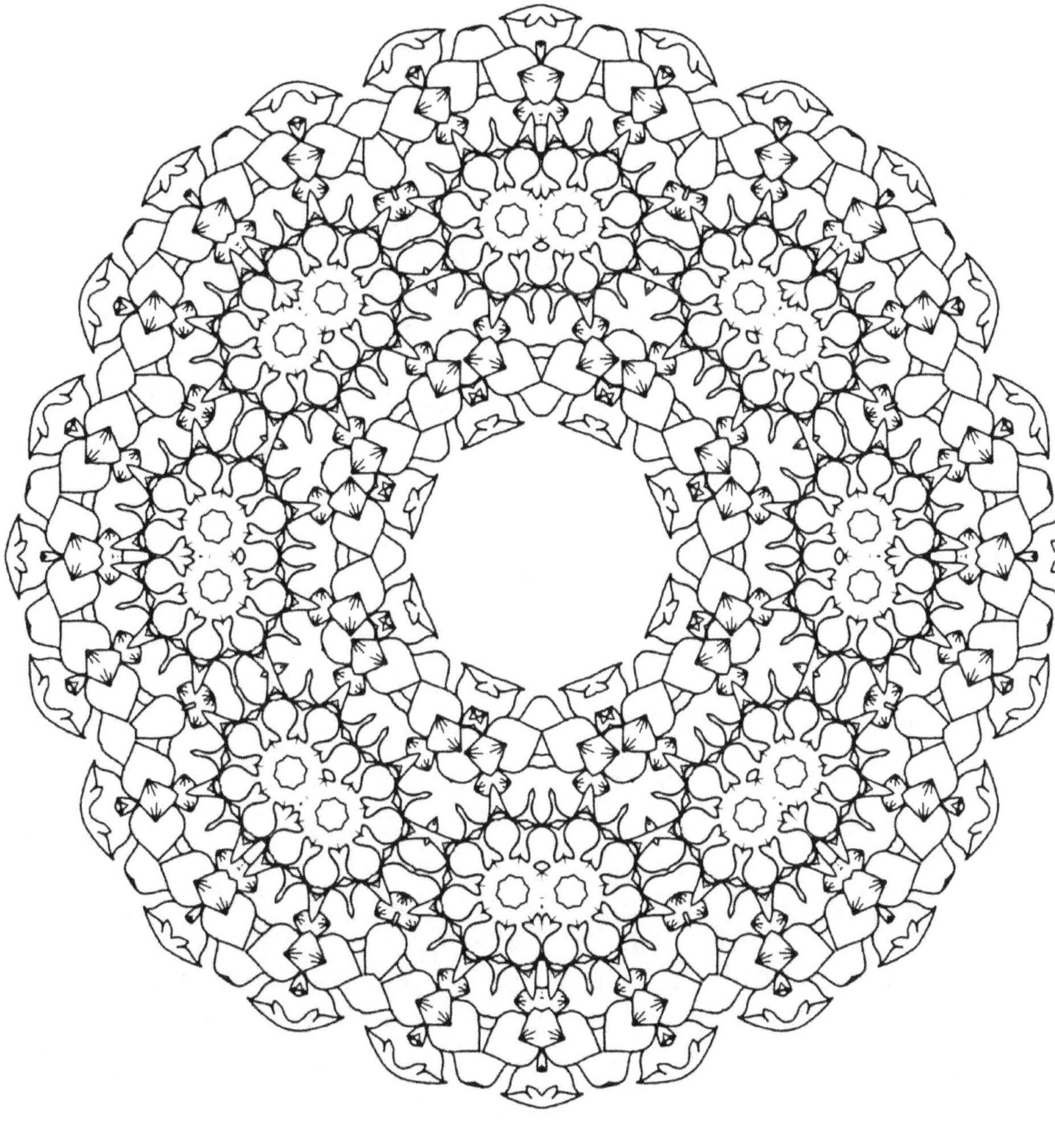

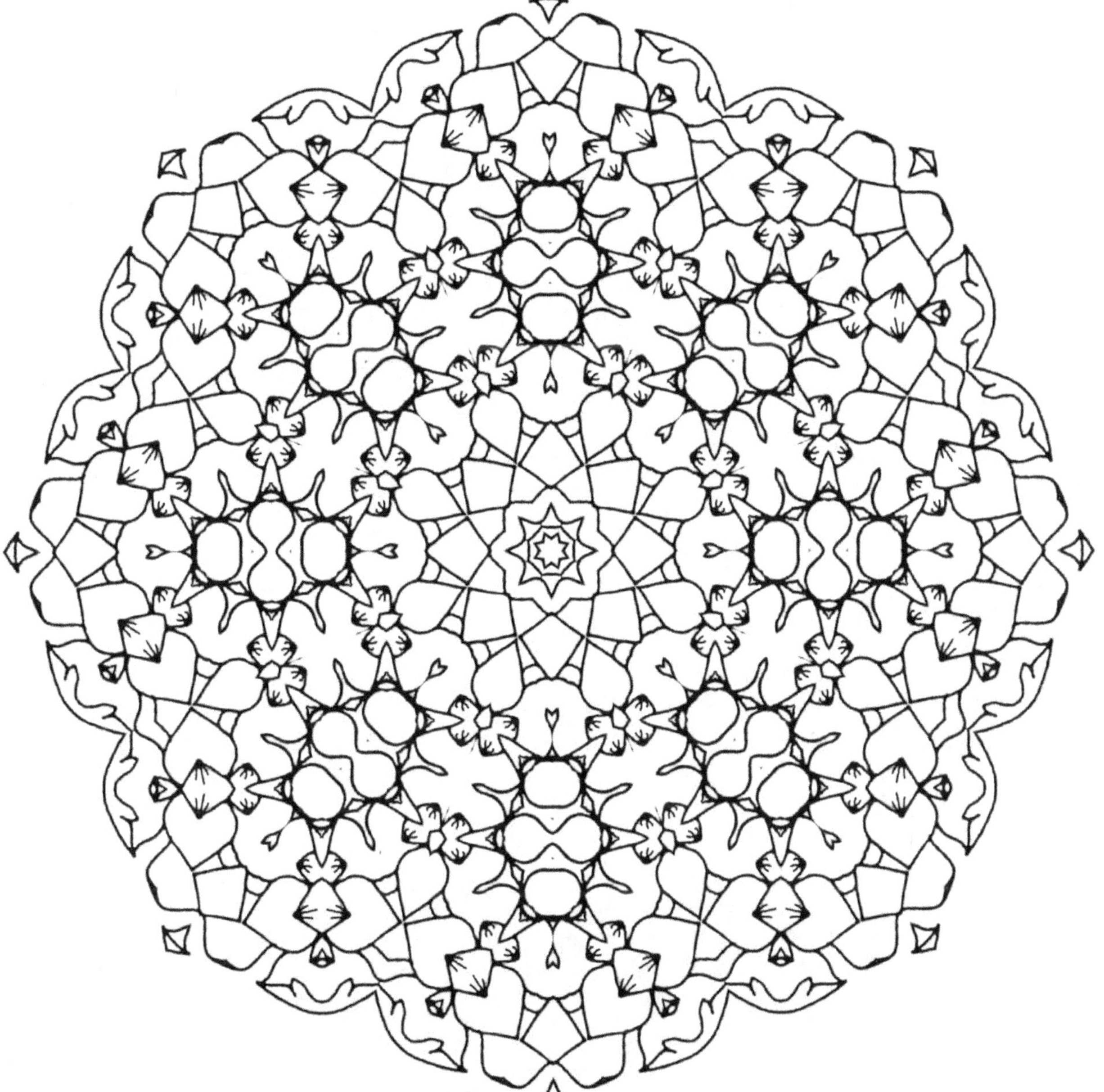

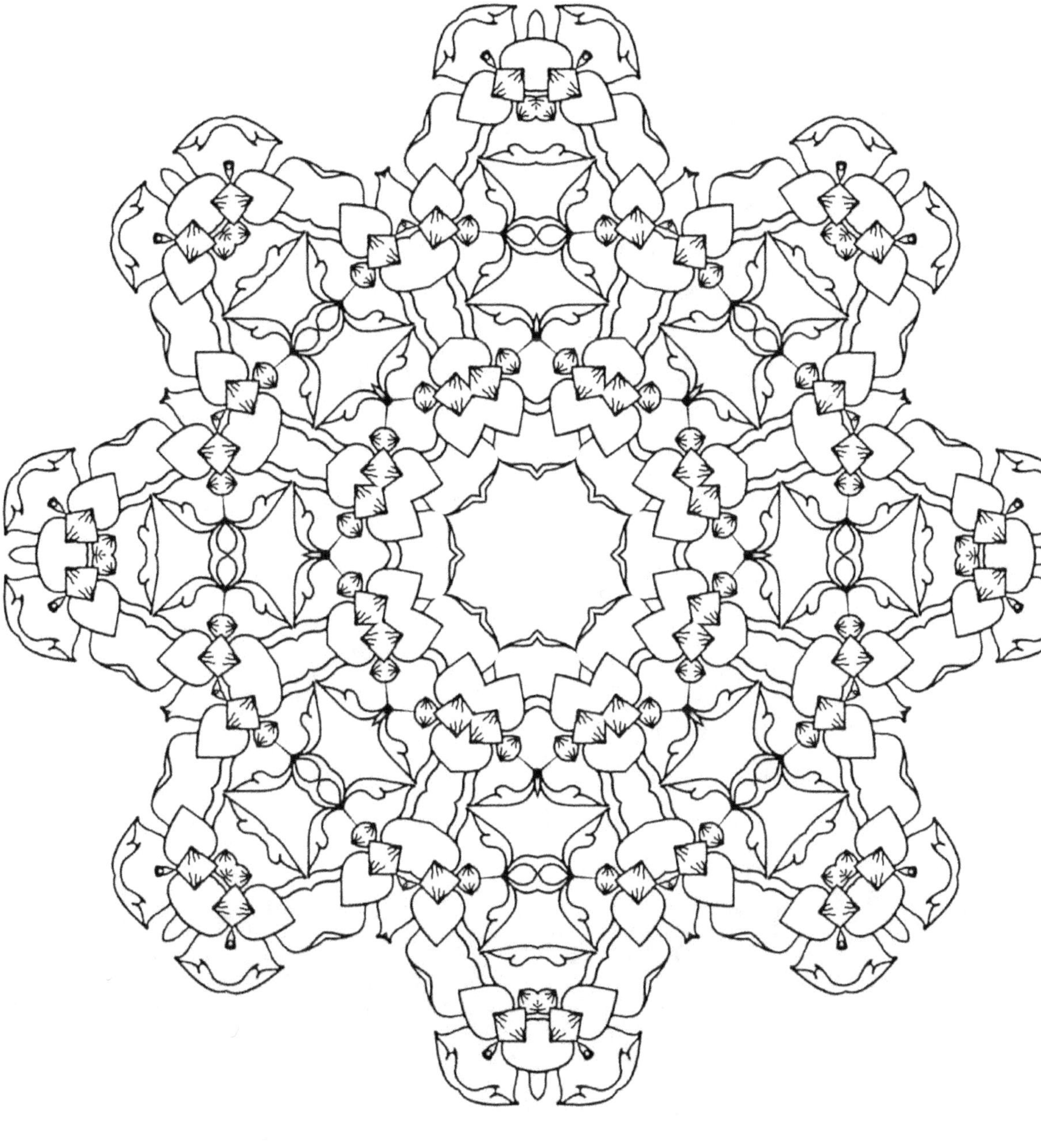

Thank you

www.ingramcontent.com/pod-product-compliance
Lightning Source LLC
Chambersburg PA
CBHW051946280526
45789CB00009B/3192
9781541256415